FAITH ARISING

FAITH ARISING

Finding the Warrior within and the
Willingness to Explore, Grow, and Arise

T. I. Frazier

FAITH ARISING

Copyright © 2022 by T. I. Frazier

Paperback ISBN: 979-8-9859038-9-8

eBook ISBN: 979-8-9859038-0-5

Typeset by Geoffrey Stone

Cover design by Danna Mathias Steele

Printed in the United States of America

To honor and to serve you, the reader. May you see my heart, my vulnerability and learn a bit about why I fell in love with God.

I pray that out of his glorious riches he may strengthen you with power through his Spirit in your inner being, so that Christ may dwell in your hearts through faith. And I pray that you, being rooted and established in love, may have power, together with all the Lord's holy people, to grasp how wide and long and high and deep is the love of Christ, and to know this love that surpasses knowledge—that you may be filled to the measure of all the fullness of God.

—Ephesians 3:16-19

Contents

INVITATION

Faith Arising explores the process that helped me create context for my faith story. As you read, I hope you find parts of my journey to which you can relate. I don't expect everything that has worked for me to be a solution for you, although you may find tools, ideas, and "aha moments" for your own faith story. I invite you to critically examine key moments in your life where you felt lost, heartbroken, inspired, challenged, courageous, overwhelmed, and at peace.

I have had a life filled with joyous experiences and am eternally grateful for all the incredible blessings. I have had communities come along beside me in moments of despair. I would be remiss if I didn't mention my African brothers in Christ, my brothers-in-arms, my family, and those who have adopted me into their family as if I were their own.

In this book, however, I explore the limiting beliefs that held me back, the hardships I faced, and the moments of shame. I am ultimately responsible for getting up and taking ownership of who I am and who I am to become; to find a way to go beyond the broken moments and arise.

This story is for everyone! Maybe you can relate to me directly regarding the growth stages and faith development. Perhaps you see your son, daughter, brother, sister, employee, colleague, or friend. I invite you to investigate your faith with me and ask some of the questions I considered to strengthen my resolve. Questions like, How do I define my faith? What gave me resilience when I fell apart, became discouraged, or suffered? How did I navigate difficult relationships? What mechanism inside of me caused me to arise?

The ideas shared in Faith Arising are based on Christian teachings. I am unapologetically Christian, although I considered deeply how to discuss and provide a field manual on faith without alienating those who may be developing their understanding and how they align themselves to religious ideas. I am not attempting to create an apologetic on Christian thought. Instead, I hope you can consider the teachings here more as suggestions and ideas of what has worked well for me. It's okay to agree with me, disagree with me, and wrestle with ideas. The questioning of faith is where faith begins, and I am confident the resulting growth will be valuable.

INTRODUCTION

Now faith is confidence in what we hope for and assurance about what we do not see. This is what the ancients were commended for. By faith we understand that the universe was formed at God's command, so that what is seen was not made out of what was visible

—Hebrews 11:1-3 NIV

The story of the Israelites in the Bible is one where they suffered, were challenged, and enslaved for many generations. Some of these generations did not see God's promises of a future and abundance fulfilled. However, their hope was in God regardless.

Growing up this challenged me because I couldn't understand why a community of people would hold steadfast to God and perhaps spend their entire life waiting for God to deliver. As an American I have bought into the idea of freedom, the ability to pursue my desires and dreams. I've heard messages about finding my purpose, drive, and creating a life. In contrast, I also saw communities showing expressions of generational oppression by being enslaved to their addictions, poor belief patterns, and abusive relationships. I saw the tired, the weak, and the lonely.

Now, those who believe we can manifest our own lives, which I do as well, might be challenged by the above scenario. We might ask, Was God delaying the Israelites from experiencing the future promised? Why couldn't they have been able to change their circumstances? Did something go wrong?

While I think it is tempting to blame God for the circumstances the Israelites found themselves in, the Bible was not shy to express how God's people were also responsible for getting themselves into their predicaments. The theme of their story, however, was the development of their faith, being victorious, and crossing the threshold into living in God's promises. The change in their circumstances could not have been made visible with the absence of faith.

Like the Israelites, I needed to develop my own faith. I needed to learn about faith, develop it, and discover how to make it my own. Initially, my faith and belief system came from my parents. Eventually, as I grew older, I recognized that in order to fully come into my own as a man, I needed to establish my own faith. This realization did not come from the pursuit of faith, but from a question deep within me and where this story begins.

The simple question: When do you become a man? It never seemed clear, and it became tedious to obtain answers. Despite all my achievements, awards, and acquired life skills, I desired to know the truth concerning this question. Am I a man when I get that promotion, go to that college, or hit a particular age? Am I a man when I become a husband or father or lose my virginity? Did I become a man at that point?

There are a lot of grown-up boys in this world right now who are successful with a lot of money and all other things, but never took ownership of their life, their faith, and convictions. They may even have lots of dough and the goodies of life. But the pertinent questions we must each ask ourselves regarding our own ship: Is it a sinking one or can it stand the test of time? Can it resist the stress of storms, or is it the one that will put us in a situation where we will need to swim our way out of the raging seas of life in peril of drowning?

For some, the ship they are sailing on, inherited or not, whether they are grown-ups or not, is what I will call a duct-tape ship. Some made theirs out of cardboard, already set up to sink.

Owning your faith does not mean you won't experience the turbulence of life. It means that your faith is established or rooted in the indestructible essence from which humanity was born. It means getting up and choosing to be a leader even when it seems like your inner strength is gone.

Some may confuse this with the idea of resiliency. What tends to be taught about resiliency projects this idea of your ability to bounce back from adverse circumstances, which connotes that you are already prepared for tough situations. Not only that, but you also expect the beauty of things that will come after tough situations have passed.

What I prescribe is a threshold of faith acquired through uncertainty and fear, but more importantly, love, which drives us to a place where the character of our being thrives despite outward circumstances.

Faith and how to apply this idea of taking ownership of life can be ambiguous and challenging without a map to help discern our situations, the places in life we find ourselves, and what steps we can take in the moments we experience destruction and confusion.

There are seven growth phases or stages I believe were essential in supporting me to achieve this. As I learned more about the stages I recognize that there are times when I experience some of the stages again. With new awareness, however, I was able to embrace the step I was on with clarity and discernment.

The seven growth stages on how to develop our faith are:

1. Soil
2. Seed
3. Roots
4. Trunk
5. Branches
6. Fruit
7. Pruning

When we reach the threshold of faith, we obtain confidence in a deeper web of connectivity in life. Our source of energy is no longer predicated on one's own inner strength, but from the universe, God, the source of life itself. It is about thriving and independently creating. This is where we can invite our families and teach our sons and daughters how to take ownership of their own faith, dreams, and lives.

1
SOIL

In the beginning, God spoke. As a result of God speaking, there was a frequency. Then sound came to be, and something emerged. But before the sound, there was nothing. In the same way, before the seeds of life and faith or whatever humanity resides in us, there was also nothing.

Before something grew inside us and the breaking forth of things from within to outside occurred, there was nothing, just like in the beginning. We often talk about the metaphor of planting seeds in people's lives, but the truth is, we need the soil first for the seeds to find expression.

What exists in our lives before seeds grow within it? We do. So, in this sense, we are nutritious dirt designed to have seeds planted in us before creation can grow from us.

Now, let's consider that sometimes we feel emptiness to the extent we hit rock bottom. If I'm to define it, hitting rock bottom is the soil. After hitting rock bottom, some people become hopeless to the extent that they do not see a way out. Others find getting up from there challenging. They think to themselves, "Okay, I have hit rock bottom, and I'm just going to stay down here." That was my state some years back. There was no magical way of getting better. In fact, I didn't want to get better. I felt if I did get better, they would just knock me down again. "Nobody wants me to get better; so, why try in the first place?"

That's how I felt in corporate America for a long time. I would get up, conquer my situation, only to get knocked down again. It was like, "What is the point in getting better? Why am I fighting? Let me just stay down—no need to fight anymore. I'm tired."

When we get to those moments in life, we can recognize them as soil. It is not compulsory that there should be a purpose, mission, or drive at that moment. That's not the focus; our aim should be how to prepare the soil, or better yet, prepare our soul.

In our moments of emptiness, when there is nothing and we think God is gone, when everything stays silent and we have reached a sure place in our empty selves (some call it solace, peace, or cold loneliness), our job at that distinct moment is to prepare the soil. When we prepare that soil, that's when we begin to have an intimate relationship with something deeper within ourselves.

Preparing the soil includes asking the questions, what are you feeding yourself in those moments? What are you bringing into yourself? Whatever you bring into yourself becomes the seed that births and gives existence of what is to come.

Preparing the soil is the most powerful point of meditation. It is the thud at the bottom of the well. It is the sound in the darkness that goes boom, the big bang inside ourselves where everything concerning our nothingness condenses into the seed that will give birth to the power which is the essence of our soul.

We must not misinterpret this step because the misinterpretation will lead us astray, and we will actually dismantle the process rather than take up what we've cultivated and created. For example, self-talk which limits our vision of the future has the potential to unravel the works of compounding nutrition within our soil, or perhaps interweaves fear or a spirit of destruction within the seeds we create.

To illustrate, I recall events that had an impact on limiting my vision of myself over many years. In high school I was a tremendous athlete, recognized for my achievements in track and field. I had jumped nearly twenty-four feet in the long jump my senior year, placing me among the best in the nation. In college I expected to do even greater, however, after being injured most of my freshmen year, I had to have surgery on both my knees. This injury was more than just an injury. It was a shot to my ego and my identity. It was a rock-bottom moment for me—an athlete no longer in the spotlight, no longer proving to the world my superior strength and ability.

While some may have recovered and gone on to rejoin the sport they loved, I did not. Compounded by being at a school where I experienced active discrimination, loneliness, and now a loss of identity, I shrunk into myself.

I still remember the night in my dorm room, when people were yelling racial slurs outside and students shattered light bulbs by throwing them against my window. Disillusioned, feelings of hopelessness drove me to an addiction of isolation. I fed my soul fear, hurt, and other lies, which later became self-inflicted prophecies of shame and defeat. I turned to ways of escaping life rather than being an active participant in creating it. My sense of hurt and fear defined my version of identity at the time.

That moment when I hit rock bottom, I witnessed the sense that my heart collapsed inward, and with that sense of implosion also came an external explosion of my passions. Put simply, it is a little bit like what happens when you bite into an orange. When you bite an orange, what happens? Juice comes out. The implosion creates an explosion of juice.

Once we have collected feelings, thoughts, and ideas in the emptiness, the intensity of these things implodes, and a seed is born. A seed will nearly implode on itself before the explosion of life when the roots begin to take form.

Concerning our own circumstances, we often misperceive what happens inside of us by thinking of implosion as death. Instead, such a situation actually allows us to explore and stretch our roots, which are the very foundation of growth in taking ownership of our lives.

Consider when my surgery occurred, what might have happened if I had chosen in that emptiness to meditate on healing? Or if I had taken the time to journal or read an inspiring novel? Imagine if I had surrounded myself with new friendships or taken the time that I would have been training to explore new goals, opportunities, and dreams. What if I had chosen to recognize my feelings of hurt, and in the intensity of feelings, chosen to cry? What if, within that explosion of emotion, I had allowed a seed to be born?

In the soil phase we collect nutrition and bring it into our souls to later implode, then explode into a seed. Another way of understanding this collection in the moment of emptiness, people find themselves saying I need to ask Jesus into my life; I needed to bring something into my soil or soul. When my heart was broken, I needed something to hold onto. That's the idea.

Often, we return to the empty soil state rather than proceeding to the seed and to the roots. We abandon the process. We abandon the growing seeds, thereby going back to being nothing. We should know that the implosion is the start of life, which I refer to as the birth of love. It may be hard to accept that within pain and anger we can also manifest growth and love.

Questions to Ask Yourself

What were some of the best lessons you learned or are learning in your rock-bottom moments?

What did you find you had to take responsibility for in these moments?

What did you find you were grateful for in these situations?

2
SEEDS

Life occurs when something is planted. For instance, if you look at land that has been charred by lava due to volcanic activity, over the years it begins to start growing grass, plants, and all other wonderful vegetation. The question is, where did the life come from? From the soil and through the mysteries of life, seeds find themselves awakening.

Now consider the implosion that creates life, inside the abyss and emptiness we once felt. This is the seed which can be understood as our passions, our love. When we have condensed all that is around us, the implosion brings with it an expression of love that is born inside. Think of all the seedlings of life inside you waiting to emerge from the darkness and grow into a healthy life.

When I reflect on my own story, my empty times of immense pain when I lost hope and faith, I see how I destroyed the many seeds of life/love that had the ability to emerge. Instead of bringing joy into my heart to nurture my soil, I agonized in pain and suffering. I focused all my attention on pain, and in that choice, I would say I attracted more pain into my life.

A Challenging Time

At the end of the summer after I had graduated from college, I was excited about a new job offer. The weekend before starting in the new role, however, I doubled over in immense pain I had never experienced. I went to urgent care only to be sent home with pain medicine. I was told it was probably a kidney stone, and I would be fine once it passed. Convinced there was something really wrong, I had a friend drive me to the hospital a few days later. The moment I arrived, I collapsed in the waiting room from the sheer pain. I don't remember exactly what happened next, but I recall waking up to a doctor in front of me explaining that I needed to go into immediate surgery. My appendix had ruptured, and I had become septic. Doctors expected that they would need to remove parts of my small and large intestines as well. My friend tried to comfort me, explaining it was a small surgery and not a big deal.

I woke up after surgery disoriented, confused, and moaning in pain. I leaned over the bed, expelling a black liquid from both sides of my body. Nurses rushed in and immediately gave me a powerful pain drug. This happened again and again and again. At one point they had pumped so many drugs into my system I hallucinated, seeing bats coming out of people's mouths like in a horror movie. I remember trying to escape through the window and it took multiple people to bring me back into the room.

I was in the hospital for over two weeks. I ended up needing a second surgery, and they pumped nearly ten liters of bacteria out of my body. I lost almost fifty pounds and could hardly stand. Where my chest and pectoral muscle once were, you could see my rib bones all the way to my collar bone.

I wish I could say that was rock bottom, but things continued to compound. I didn't have health insurance. I was in debt, and I also lost the job that I had just been offered. I tried to work almost immediately when I got out of the hospital, in fear of not having enough money to live. Still sick and weak, I was not performing up to the task. They terminated me within thirty days. As a young man who didn't have his family in town, I looked to people around me for support. To my surprise, many people said things like, "Where is your family? Go home to them," or "Why don't you just file bankruptcy?" Others insisted, "Just get a job."

All these could be valid points for many, but for me, they were not realistic options. I lived thousands of miles away from my parents; my dad struggled with a disease and was on disability. It was a recession and even when I applied at a fast-food restaurant, I was told I was overqualified. I refused to file for bankruptcy because I couldn't understand why fifteen days of my life in the hospital should define the next seven years of my financial opportunities.

A hundred thousand dollars in debt, with no job, and a car with almost no gas, I lived in an apartment where I couldn't turn on the heat because I knew I wouldn't be able to pay the bill. I had frost inside the apartment. I remember walking to the store and buying one little candle. At night I would put on all my clothes and light the candle. I never realized how powerful one candle could be, but it made a big difference in how hot my bedroom felt.

I recall saying, "God, have mercy on me!" And at that very moment, I also questioned, "What if the worst pain and suffering I am experiencing is mercy?" I remember asking myself, "Is God going to save me?"

In the darkness, feeling betrayed by friends, I spouted negative thoughts to myself. I was angry, screaming for help. Could anyone hear me?

My sense of safety and security were stripped away. Over the next several months, I wandered from churches to food pantries applying for jobs, looking for shelter, and seemingly getting nowhere. A moment of hope was met with a double dose of despair. My car would break down and need expensive fixes, which my parents were able to help with. I ate sardines from the can, which I would open with a knife. I got a free trial gym membership and would change the dates on the card, so I could shower and stay warm.

I waited around for God to show up, and He seemingly didn't. So, what do you do when God doesn't show up?

I began to understand what it meant to be the captain of your own ship. You don't wait for someone to show up. You try something different. You try something new, and you don't try something out of desperation. You don't seek something out of naivety (openness of your heart) that ends up becoming a scam. No. You bring into yourself the resources of what you have been blessed with. I was waiting for God when He had already placed the nutrition, skills, tools, and opportunities I needed in my life, but I didn't recognize them.

Instead, I stayed in a place of despair, tearing down what was being built inside of me in the confusion and darkness.

What Changed?

First, I accepted what took place. Next, I allowed myself to dream of what I really wanted in that moment. I didn't want to be saved. I wanted to rise up and be stronger than any "storm" that came my way. I wanted to feel loved, appreciated, and safe.

The next step: I asked myself a simple question: "What assets do you have right now?" My answer—time. Then I challenged myself and said, "What are you going to do with all this time?"

It's hard to describe exactly what took place, but I began to attract into my life ideas that grew into seeds of possibilities, which grew into little buds of opportunities. I found God inside of me instead of where I was looking all around me. By imploding into myself under the immense pressure of my life circumstances, what squeezed out of me were thoughts that turned into the seeds of necessary growth. It was the first insight and hint of understanding my identity as a human. At first, I didn't understand. I stayed broken in the abyss. But when I allowed myself to question and explore the possibilities, I was able to bring into myself all that was inside me and around me.

Questions to Ask Yourself

What questions are you asking yourself to promote personal growth?

What seeds have you noticed growing in your life?

3
ROOTS

This is the third key phase in the development of faith, strength, endurance, and understanding—the roots. This is the part I call the relationship, learning God or the universe. This includes adventure stories of experiencing how the universe functions and moves in life. This is where we create the inter-connected foundation of understanding and how those under-standings shape our growth.

Growing up in a Christian family I was told by the church to "be like Jesus." So, I thought that when I experienced storms in life, by just closing my eyes and saying like Jesus, "Storm, be still," the storms of life would vanish. Oh, how my bubble was burst when I realized it doesn't happen that way. I had to be okay with living in the storm. It wasn't a stormy night; it was a stormy life, and I had to accept living with that every day. I had to admit that my truth in the moment might mean being okay that I couldn't get up or didn't feel deter-mined.

It is hard to recognize what you are doing when your life feels like an eternal darkness. Like a miner searching for gold,

I asked myself, "What am I mining in my life? Do I just need to stick with something long enough until I find gold? Or am I digging in the wrong spot?" You can't know all these answers while in the dark. I probably dug in some areas that if I stuck there long enough, I might have been a multi-millionaire today. But there are also those spots where I probably should have never been digging in the first place.

This is the discovery and development of the foundation—the foundation where you learn how to live in the storm and find the seeds the winds bring to you, the opportunities the universe presents. While in the roots phase, you learn how to pay attention and how to ask and receive that which God/the universe can provide.

The biggest secret I learned here was to go from knowing something in my head to having my beliefs rooted in my heart. It is about how I learned to be in an experience with everything around me and recognize how I am truly connected with my environment.

The big question here is, How do you go from just your head or just your heart to finding cohesion between the two? I found that I am the most powerful when my heart and mind are not in conflict with one another. Words like *empathy, compassion, faith,* and *love* are associated with root development and are words that enforce the concept of unison: one mind, one heart, and one goal.

In contrast, when there was a lack of unison in me, I spent more time battling internal debates, trapped between achieving my dreams and justifying the betrayal of my heart. Such betrayals can lead to sin and separation. We experience defeats in life when isolated.

Empathy

People often confuse empathy and sympathy. While sympathy is sharing in the feelings of someone else, empathy is understanding the feelings of someone else—understanding and relating with others when they are experiencing the emptiness of themselves, understanding the pain and feelings of loss, understanding the feelings of being shipwrecked or the feelings of starting over. You can also feel empathy during celebration, a victory, the feeling you get when you see your favorite team win the championship by overcoming seemingly impossible feats.

Empathy allows us to resonate or vibrate at the same level of those experiencing what we want to feel. What we want to feel is a frequency we give out like a radio wave, and what we receive back is the same feeling in return. For those experiencing the negative things in life, our empathy allows for us to provide the energy they lack.

Think of it like trees or vegetation planted near one another. Their roots entangle underground, allowing both to thrive and receive all the soil has to offer. The language of the roots allows them to share what each one needs, and they all give up something that becomes enough for all to go through a time of drought or disease.

The challenge and reward in showing empathy is that this process of caring and connecting with others should change you. It should help direct your growth and the pillars of understandings you have, the truths of the world you uphold. Examples of change that comes from empathy may include: I might need to reimagine my contextual understanding of God or what life is. I may need to understand my relationship, marriage, children, or who I am as a spouse differently.

Compassion

Compassion adds a layer to empathy, which is the desire to help. A key to lifting the veil off compassion is recognizing its relationship with the word *suffering*. If you choose to look up the etymology of compassion, a synonym is *suffering*.

During my freshman year of high school, we were required to run a mile as a test for physical fitness. For me, I was excited and filled with nerves every time. I was energized. I couldn't wait to beat my best time again, to compete and strive to dominate my peers. For others, it was the worst day. Some would try to hide in the locker room or get a sick slip, anything to get out of running.

On this one occasion, the gym teacher rushed us onto the track as quickly as possible as it was scheduled to rain. I stepped onto the track, jockeying for position, and the gun went off. I remember finishing with a blistering time of four minutes, forty-eight seconds. I was told to go back in as the rain was already starting to come down.

Instead, I stayed out cheering my friends on but also slightly gloating as I wanted to make sure they saw I was done already. Soon the bulk of the class had completed the run and just in time. The rain went from drizzling to what would soon be one of those drenching rains where you can hardly see twenty feet in front of you. As people began to go in, I turned to go with them, but then I heard a classmate call out his lap number, "lap three." That meant he had completed only two laps. I started to account for all the members of my class, and I realized he was the last one.

Without thought, I jumped back on the track and started jogging. My eyes were nearly closed shut from all the water pouring down, my sweatpants were falling off my waist with every splatter of my foot hitting the ground. I found my class-mate and yelled out, "I can't run for you, but I can run with you." There was a silent acknowledgment as I ran beside him.

At first, I yelled words of encouragement, trying to moti-vate my classmate to keep going. Painfully slow on the far side of the track, drowning in the rain and in thought, my words, my mind, and heart became silent. I never knew how it felt to be the last one where no one was there to cheer you on. I never knew what it meant for the goal to be not to win, but to just finish. I was angry. I felt invisible and hurt that no one else was there.

By the last lap, the "I" feelings disappeared and in its place was the rhythm of my feet and his running together, the rhythm of our inhaling and exhaling in unison. I left "I" in the rain at the finish line, and we went back into the locker room together.

Faith

While this book is dedicated to the development and process of faith arising, faith is part of the roots, the foundation of our thoughts unseen but essential for establishing the pillars of our life's work. I want to go back to that Scripture I used, which says, "Now faith is confidence in what we hope for and assurance about what we do not see" (Heb. 11:1 NIV). Do I have assurance about what I do not see? We hope, and we have faith and confidence in something greater than ourselves. How do we become confident in something we don't see? Consider the years of bondage the Israelites or any other enslaved people endure. How many years were they enslaved? How many years did they toil without experiencing the fruits of their labor?

If you choose to read the story in the book of Hebrews and check out some of the people mentioned, you can't help but ask, "How much did these people sacrifice in their lives for a promise that wasn't theirs?" These people lived a life paving a road for a destination they would never see. And they didn't do it for themselves, they literally did it for the next generation and the generations to follow.

God gave them a vision so great that it was far beyond what they would ever experience. That's the character of a true warrior and dedicated servant because they were committed to planting generational seeds and working on generational soil. They dedicated their lives to that which is incredible.

Imagine what it takes to dedicate yourself to such an agenda. As a Black and Puerto Rican man experiencing certain levels of discrimination and prejudice in life and within corporate America, I fight every day to create a new vision, knowing that somehow, even my failures may be the foundation of opportunities for later generations.

Faith also stems from our ancestral roots. They are the voices inside us that are deeper than what we may be aware of. It's those roots and foundations that begin our story because when we don't have our own roots, we hold on to the roots of the people around us. This is what it means to plant our-selves spiritually next to other people.

My wife has her own journey; I have mine. But when you're planted close spiritually, you get to tie into the web of roots in the ground. There is a reason why things planted next to each other grow better, with appropriate space, of course. As they grow intricately woven into one another, they inter-lock. I would suggest that through empathy, compassion, and faith we adopt a new version of family roots.

In several places in the New Testament there is the idea of God adopting everybody and not just the Hebrews. How I understand this is that God is saying, You're now intertwined in My root system. That's special because you now have access to the living waters that exist in God's root system. Now you are intertwined underground with the whole network where you can always live, breathe, and grow.

Love

I believe that love is the root of our humanity and design. There are two key thoughts in the Bible: (1) that God is love, and (2) that we are made in the image of God. Therefore, we could conclude that we are made in the image of love.

If you accepted this identity as your own, what would that mean to you? When you evaluate the way you speak to the people in your life, are you communicating out of the identity of love? Or maybe you communicate something different, like fear, worry, and destruction.

When we choose to communicate out of any other spirit or energy that is not love, we have accepted a false truth or belief. These false beliefs are what create the illusion of separation and thus separation from the divine. Roots are about being connected to the resources for growth, the living waters which nurture healthy living. Becoming aware of how we love and the nurturing resources through which we experience love allows for us to tap into what we need to grow healthy spirit-led lives.

Love Stories

In my late twenties I married a beautiful woman who had won my heart, and in exchange, I promised myself to her. Despite our ages, we were both still learning and discovering our identity and desires in life. As a man I was learning the new role of husband and in what ways I contribute to a marriage. I was also learning about myself and the career path I chose to develop. Likewise, she was learning how to contribute to a marriage and her career path.

Within two months we had the exciting experience of becoming pregnant. How quickly our imaginations, thoughts, and desires changed course. Hormones were changing; emotions were elevated. Even now as I remember, cold chills run through my body and my heart sinks as I think about the moment we recognized an early miscarriage taking place. How can I explain how that felt? How can I tell you about the emotions when I would experience this loss nine more times? An endless numb winter of my soul glazed over my heart. I felt anger and confusion, fumbling in the dark while shrinking inside of myself where no cry for help could be heard. Love eroded into fermented toxic waste. Confusion and self-preservation drove both of us to act out our pain, only inflicting more pain on ourselves and on each other.

I can't speak for the woman and her experiences, but I can tell you that losing ten unborn children and simultaneously watching myself lose the love of my life brought me to an unrecognizable version of me. I sought isolation, cut off from the world, from love, from life or any root connection. I searched deep within to find the warrior inside me, the one who served with integrity and honor, the one with the mindset I took on when ready to kill or die for my country. I couldn't find that man. I closed my eyes and was swept out to sea, shipwrecked, abandoning my destiny. And where was love? It was an abandoned idea, a failed experiment.

In this part of my life, I accepted false truths, including false ideas about love. I felt bound to perpetual failure, attracting more pain. I accepted bad habits and inhibition. I also became easily persuaded by the web of lies that exists within culture, and in the web of lies, deceitfulness erodes our understanding of faith and our ability to accept new truths or attract new beginnings.

The second story of love comes right after my divorce. I bought a home in the woods and lived alone, just me and my dog, Rocky. I was lonely and still very angry with life. I would spend my weekends chopping wood, thoughts festering in my mind. I had insomnia and felt extremely tired. Most days I was not motivated to go to the job but I would be forced awake by a relentless, hungry dog who literally would drag me out of my bed. Looking at the day and not knowing what I would do at home, I went to work out of routine. Like a good actor, I would put on the disposition of a happy, energetic man while secretly hoping some type of accident would happen every time I went home, so I wouldn't have to keep living.

Like fool's gold, there was a woman I met that seemed to shine. I was mesmerized. She danced around my soul, filling the holes and brokenness. The wisdom of my life told me that it made no sense to get involved. However, the careless reckless version of me was what I allowed to dictate my life. I was in love, and she was the answer. Out of respect for the woman and the intent of the story I cannot share her situation, thoughts, or emotions. What I can say is she captured my attention, and in the intense desires of a vulnerable, isolated heart, our intimacy led to her becoming pregnant.

When the women chose to abort, my soul left my body. Besides the complete loss of my spirit, I now carried the burden of shame and guilt. Did it matter that I fought with every ounce of myself to change her mind? I still wore the invisible burden shackled to the bottom of the ocean, suffocating in my own muffled cries.

A Few Thoughts

I hope you can recognize two deceptions that took place in these stories. One is that we can't discern truth, neither can we recognize love because we are entangled and broken. I chose to remain isolated instead of drawing sustenance from the community and people connected in my root system.

The second failure is the misperception or deception that the people, places, or things I reached out to in my life were living waters. Instead, these things created something that appeared to be a root system which was ultimately designed to fail because it was not connected to that deeper network.

There is a way to discern these things. There is a way to avoid the perpetual darkness of the soul where you end up repeatedly rebuilding and getting nowhere. I needed once again to start from the emptiness, the nothing. The reason I was there again was because my root system failed to continue to provide the nutrition I needed to grow strong. Also, my soil failed to have the nutrition inside of it because I was not seeking to surround myself with positive ingredients to manifest and create healthy seeds.

To change the stuff we attract in life, we need to give off a new frequency. In doing so, we will no longer be bound by the experiences we've had but will practice healthy patterns and attract something new. We can't do that if we don't acknowledge the darkness and release ourselves from old patterns, which really means letting ourselves go in a sense. That's why I speak about it so much because it's 100 percent essential for our growth.

I've heard it said that in life we either communicate love or fear. Fear bound me to suffering, and I repeated the behaviors that attracted more fear.

When we are afraid, we hold on to things even if it is unhealthy. At that point, we don't discriminate. When we're hungry enough, whether we're given chips or vegetables, we don't discriminate; we just want to eat. Our appetite begins to rule our lives rather than allowing for change. To attract goodness, or should I say to truly manifest goodness, we need our actions to match our passions and love, and let those things be the vision of our souls.

Fear of repeating behaviors or being hurt by the same type of people in our lives is driven by a lack of forgiveness. Love is the act of forgiving or the act of releasing the responsibility another has to heal you. In the story of the second woman, I knew that if any version of me was to survive that last straw, I was going to need to forgive her and myself by allowing unmerited favor to rewrite my heart's disposition. This is my definition of grace, which releases us from even the damage and fate we wish upon ourselves and others.

Years later, the woman and I reconciled the pain, choosing to forgive each other for what parts we were responsible for and choosing grace for one another. Grace allows healing inside of us and is a crucial aspect of the forgiveness process. I'm so grateful there is grace and on-going healing in areas of my life that are still vulnerable to this day.

I'm convinced that the child lost was a beautiful baby girl. In my process of accepting what took place, the woman and I named her Grace. To accept what took place is to accept Grace in our lives, and even though she didn't land on this Earth, she is forever a part of my soul, forever a part of my life.

I chose to let these events form my decisions, and I choose to love everybody, whether it's to have mercy and grace, or to show empathy and compassion through understanding what "those parts" of your story can look like. It's okay to choose love in those moments, because that's the only way you're going to heal, and that's the only way that someone else can heal.

Some wounds might stay there forever, but every time I stumble upon them, instead of pouring salt in them, I pour a little love. After war and bloodshed on a field, people go back years later and plant trees. After the loss, no matter how it transpired, I hope I inspire you to plant a tree of grace, love, power, and beauty in those spaces.

October 15 is Pregnancy & Infant Loss Remembrance Day. I take that day very seriously to continue to heal in that area of my life. Though I've now been blessed with a beautiful marriage and with the joy of my son, I don't take that for granted.

Questions to Ask Yourself

In what new ways can you express empathy in your life?

What people, places, or things do you have compassion for in your life? How do you express that compassion?

What new visions in faith are you creating or dedicating yourself to?

What ways have you seen yourself communicate fear instead of love? How can you make a change to express what you desire?

4
TRUNK

After the two love stories I shared with you, I lost all drive and ambition. I had gained an immense amount of weight. I lived as a victim to my life. Would you blame me? What was I living for? Where was my tenacity, drive, and sense of being empowered? Did God desert me? Where was the warrior deep within? While this was very much an empty moment, I had a lot of deserted seeds in my heart. This time I wasn't starting from scratch but from one of the lowest points in my life. The circumstances might have been different, but I was familiar with that feeling when your mind spins out of control and there doesn't seem to be an exit to the merry-go-round of thoughts.

For me, I needed a routine I could rely on to push me forward even when I didn't feel driven. This routine needed to be instinctual, not something reliant. I needed an outlet for the moments where anger and other emotions wanted to seep out of me; I needed a place to pound my soul, forging it into a new instrument of faith, determination, and perseverance. This wasn't a "fake it until you make it" feeling. It was a feeling I could describe only as Faith Arising. While the word *rise* means to move from a lower state or position to a higher one, it also means to emerge and come into being.

I define *faith* as the process of discovering or rediscovering what empowers your soul to love unconditionally without waiver. It is where you take full ownership of your life, the events that took place, and choose to be dedicated to the person you desire to be. Faith is also where we stop reaching for what is outside of us and start searching within. Faith is birthed from the unseen, already existing without physical proof. It is where the seeds in our hearts emerge and become visible.

For the Christian journey, one who has asked Jesus into their heart, faith emerges from Jesus within. The seed of faith lies buried in the dirt and in our hearts, growing roots and emerging into the formation of the trunk.

The trunk is the strongest, most structurally visible aspect of a tree. It provides the foundation of strength and continued growth. The trunk connects the inner work we do in our lives and the outward expression of our passions. It is central to faith and keeps us centered on ourselves and our inner navigation system. In short, the trunk is made up of our spiritual practices, the core of who we are. These practices we perform every day. For example, the way you eat, the way you work out, your dedication to your job, and the way you love your spouse are all spiritual practices. Failing to fortify these practices allows decay to consume the most structural aspect essential for bearing branches and fruit.

These spiritual practices are the rhythm of our relationship with the universe. We may come to see extraordinary miracles take place while we practice these on our faith journey.

Why are spiritual practices so important? They are the disciplines of our heart, and the disciplines of our heart are the instruments designed to help us navigate life when our instincts and emotions may not be trustworthy. Our instruments fine-tune our evaluation and influence our directional choices. These practices and navigational tools subtly begin to steer our life's vision and the seeds manifesting themselves. It is the moment we go from "life is happening to me," to "I am steering, I am the captain of my explorations."

Like your physical body, your spirit has its own set of muscles. Without strengthening them, they deteriorate and atrophy. Unlike the body which can still wither and become diminished with age, your spirit can grow stronger. Look at the light behind some of the elders you may know. Something burns inside of them. Like a youthful secret, concerns, stresses, and worries don't bother them. Greater than just their roots, their pillar of strength is in the patterns they commit to every day.

My Spiritual Practices

In order to strengthen and grow my trunk, I started with a meditation about love, success, and abundance that I found on YouTube. I listened to it with headphones. I didn't believe a word it was saying. I couldn't imagine my life the way the video track suggested, but I still listened. I listened all day, every day. I kept my headphones on morning and night, while

I slept, while I drove, while at work. I listened until it drove me nuts, and then I kept listening. Eventually my thoughts and negative self-talk were drowning in affirmations and meditations. Slowly I started to feel like my child-like imagination was flirting with my smiles and laughs.

Out of this meditation birthed a fixation of being dedicated to the "work." I continued to feed my mind in such a way as to condition my entire being (heart, mind, and soul) to continue through the desert, where I felt like I had labored in vain, accomplishing nothing and still too thirsty to survive.

I spent days reading about brain chemistry and what practices I needed to have to reprogram the negative and perhaps even some subconscious beliefs that up until now controlled my life. I started to study the Bible not just read it. I studied human origins and looked at what the ancients believed about the essence of our identity as humans, the power of our soul, and what truly connects us to something greater. These teachings were an ancient blueprint to understanding the advanced technology of our being. It was a method to unlock the strength and drive within. I learned about the connection between hermetic principles, ancient Egypt, the Kabbalah, the Torah, the Bible, the Koran, and Tao.

While the Bible is my source of truth, reading objectively about other religion and philosophies provided insight of shared beliefs, different perspectives, and the uniqueness the story of Christ brings.

For the first time in my life, I felt limitless and in control of my destiny. The principles I was learning and practicing in my life were spiritual practices. These practices were becoming the pillars of strength that made me question in optimistic anticipation: What if I became healthy again? What if I found joy in my life? What if there is something greater meant for my life?

I believe there are times when we need to trust the practices in our lives over our senses and what we can see. Trust your training.

When I was a soldier, we trained on how to escape a vehicle in the water. They put us in a stripped-down Humvee in a pool and turned it upside-down We would have to escape the vehicle and make it to safety. During the rollover process, we learned how many people become disoriented in an accident and swim in the wrong direction, eventually drowning. We learned how to become aware in dangerous circumstances and use the things around us to determine which way we should travel in case our natural instincts might be inaccurate. Spiritual practices are just like this. What we practice every day prepares us for dangers—seen, unseen, and perhaps never experienced—to have the tools to make decisions in those circumstances.

There were other more advance trainings where flight instruments were damaged and provided inaccurate data. We had to learn to use other tools to make the right decision in critical situations. How we discern in moments like this comes from the discipline within our own practices, which allows us to know the difference. That's why training and repetition become so important. I have seen many become shipwrecked inadvertently because they have no idea how to use the instruments they possess.They have no idea whether to trust them or if the information they are receiving is accurate.

Another way of establishing spiritual practices is through sound discipline. What I mean by that is becoming aware of the frequency of your heart. It can be off or on like a radio, but you must fine-tune the vibration in order to be connected to the station you want to hear without static. If you are unaware of the frequency you're emitting, you could be fine-tuning yourself to dissonance and chaos. For example, forgiveness is a spiritual practice and a frequency. Forgiving is about releasing a situation or perhaps a person from the responsibility to heal you so that you have the opportunity to create a new frequency. This release allows you the opportunity to accept new experiences, harmonies, and sounds like love, joy, and all other positive emotions. You can't do that if you're stuck. Forgiveness, however, can be a process. That's what fine-tuning is about. Regardless of how you feel toward a situation, forgiving allows you to move on to a new frequency and desire.

Let's evaluate different spiritual practices which are the basis of faith. Some may seem obvious while others may not. My hope is that you will begin to recognize your own spiritual practices and choose to rededicate yourself to their value.

Meditation

One of the reasons meditation practices are so important is that they have two functions. One is to silence our minds to recognize the different frequencies that already exist in the background of our lives. Also, we can intentionally tune ourselves to specific frequencies and release limiting beliefs, immersing ourselves in what we truly desire. Sometimes, we're so immersed in ourselves that we can't see ourselves. We have no mirror. Therefore, because we can't see ourselves, we can't see what we're becoming or changing into.

Meditation provides the lens to see where we are, and who we are becoming. With that awareness it empowers us to review new choices and outcomes. Meditation really does that, and, as a result, it can help circumvent or remove us from the attachment of self-medicating. In my opinion, meditation is the number one way to recognize and identify tuning appropriately. The purpose is to raise our awareness levels, recognize different key aspects, and introspectively ask the faith-based questions that are the infrastructure of self-empowerment.

While this is not a how-to book on meditation, I do want to distinguish between different types of meditation. Some forms of meditation involve intentional breathing techniques. One I was taught while serving overseas is called combat or tactical breathing. The purpose was to reduce psychological stress before, during, and after intense situations. It helps to bring you back to a place of centered awareness where you can make critical potentially life-altering decisions.

I am already teaching this form to my son who is three years of age. While tantrums and crying are a part of this age, it doesn't prevent the opportunity to teach him another strategy that can be instilled early—to breath, evaluate, and then communicate what it is he wants. Some of my son's crying may not be out of feeling stress, but while he is breathing it gives me a chance to gather myself. I guess you could say I taught him the breathing techniques to keep my stress down when he cries.

Visualizing

Visions can give us understandings of the spiritual dimensions to the realities of a situation. When practicing this, you may begin by asking yourself, "What do I envision could go right concerning a situation? Or, in an ideal world, how would I like it to go down?" By answering these questions, you begin to envision it. Actor Denzel Washington said, "If you can envision it, it's proof that it already exists."

So, visualizing is a practice of creating. It is proof that something can exist even if we don't see it. The practice of visualization can happen on all different levels and playing fields. For instance, when someone journals, they may be practicing a form of visualization. In sports, visualization is heavily used. For instance, Steph Curry, a current NBA player and arguably the best shooter of all times, has both made and missed plenty of shots in basketball. However, whether he misses or makes them on a higher level than most, it is because of his visualizing and practicing.

Affirmation Statements

"I am" statements are a form of proclaiming what we desire in life. This can be a spiritual practice but is so often misused. Instead of a proclamation of power or speaking something into existence, we may turn it into some binding spell. For example, we may say things to ourselves like "I am stupid," "I am unable to ____," "I am weak," and so on. It is almost the reverse of the intention of the "I am" statement. To understand better, let us explore the origins of the "I am" affirmations.

In the Bible, when God revealed Himself to Moses, He said, "I am that I am" (Ex. 3:14 NIV). This is probably the most confusing thing grammatically that we all try to comprehend, and I love the fact that it is grammatically frustrating to fully comprehend.

As an infinity statement, the essence of "I am that I am" is all-proclaiming, calling out, and speaking into existence. When we use it for ourselves—I am peace, I am joy—we're defining a role, and embracing God's infinite supply of these characteristics. When we affirm "I am love," we are provided love from the God to give to others. I believe things can manifest in us as we begin to grow and understand that the power of the universe, God lives inside of us.

The image of God or love is inside of you.

Just saying "I am" and not putting something at the end of it can be more powerful than anything you can say next. The reason is that the proclamation allows you to tap into the frequency of all those things around you, and you now have the universe's attention.

"I am that I am" is the first part of God's name. In Hebrew, it is the very word referred to in the first of the Ten Commandments that says, "I shall not use the Lord's name in vain." I believe that to call upon the power of "I am" should not be in vain. Proclaiming should be an intentional, thoughtful practice as we recognize that when we say "I am" we are calling up the power of the universe to proclaim dominion and power.

In other words, you need to align yourself so close to the frequency of God, which is already difficult, that when you say the "I am" proclamation, everything must bow immediately because you have proclaimed dominion over it. The "I am" statement is powerful. In that proclamation we intimately connect to the universe itself.

Prayer

Prayer is the act of giving and receiving, recognizing that what you are doing is vital. By identifying what you're doing in the prayer, you fine-tune yourself to master that frequency.

When I am trying to master receiving from God or the universe, I try to adapt a form of prayer that intentionally puts me in a posture of receiving. For example, I may pray with open hands and, when finished, make the motion as if I am pouring or washing my face in the blessing.

If I am praying in a way of sending a blessing, I will reach my hand out in the direction I am sending the blessing. Often, I find that ending a prayer devoted to a certain stillness and imagining the feelings as if my prayer is answered places me in a position to experience God.

If you choose to pray, take your own steps to be aware of what you are doing. Maybe your version of prayer is having a conversation with the universe. If so, great! Conversations are good. I encourage you to be aware of your deepest desires during that time. Search your heart. Let that desire and the prayer's conversation be a version of fine-tuning your frequency.

What happens when God doesn't answer prayer? When God doesn't answer my prayers, I used to think He was shunning me. Now I consider things like maybe God is saying, "No, you desire this so much that I want you to create it and become that resource for you, your family, and everyone else around you." I have learned to be just as grateful for these moments and change my perspective to discern how God is guiding my desire to develop and make an impact.

If you visualize while you pray, here is an idea to try. Envision an empty cup representing an unfilled desire of your soul. Imagine that when you pray for certain things, God fills that cup, fulfilling your need or want. It is God's living waters pouring into those individual things you're asking for. To take this same idea a step further, imagine while you worship (through song, dance, or poetry), that God's living waters become like the floodgates overflowing. Imagine God pouring so much into your life where all your needs are met and in abundance. The song of gratitude overflows inside of you to the point that it fills all your needs abundantly.

When I visualized like this for the first time, I felt like I had entered a world of abundance. It was a place of gratitude, love, and compassion.

Devotionals

I love reading devotionals, but I often noticed I would forget all I read about halfway through the day. Seeing this as a pattern for me, I started a new method for my devotional time. I would read a devotional, then from that inspiration, I would think about the message I wanted to give others on a given day.

This became a visual concept and a proclamation of the day. It became the "I am" statement for my day and an action-based spiritual practice for me.

Here was a practice I did. I wrote down my top two spiritual practices that I wanted to focus on for the day. An example could be accountability of my emotions such as the ability to dream and meditate. Then I would ask, "Where do I start?" The beauty of doing this for me is that it unraveled and unlocked baggage I had been harboring and using to self-medicate.

My Body and Spiritual Practices

There are many teachings, thoughts, and ideas that suggest our physical well-being is intimately connected with our spiritual health. Yoga, lifting weights, running, how we eat can all impact our thoughts, self-love, and feeling of connection to the soul and the divine.

Exercise combines breathing techniques mentioned in meditation as well as visualization. Whether you imagine winning the race or your body moving in certain ways in diving or dance, you are combining meditation and visualization. Maybe exercise was really built for our hearts, minds, and bodies to practice spiritual cohesion more than just making our physiques better.

Diet is another form of spiritual practice related to the body. I find that without food discipline, the clarity of my mind and awareness can be altered. I am more sensitive to some foods than others. In order for me to function at peak ability, being aware of the food and chemicals I introduce into my body can cleanse my mind and expands my awareness of how I choose to intentionally grow in life.

Relationships and Spiritual Practices

I often find that in the initial courtship process, we show the best version of ourselves to others. As time progresses, however, the parts that are "under construction" begin to emerge. The sparks of emotions and intense feelings at first gives us energy.

Because of their strong emotions and feelings, many people desert the spiritual practices, which made them an attractive person in the beginning. Let me be clear, your source of love must be more sustainable than the fleeting intense emotions that cycle in relationships. Relationships can stir up whatever is already in the soul, but you are still responsible for doing the spiritual work to have something to stir up. Your drive, therefore, represents the deeper dedication (spiritual practice) of your life.

A Note on Mental Health

Mental health and mental disorders are real things and are a legitimate challenge. What I attracted when I was younger was a result of not having spiritual practices or a system of living. My mental health was challenged at moments, but that is very different than having a true medical diagnosis. I do believe there are great benefits to meditation and improved diets, as well as proof that spiritual practices can positively alter chemicals produced in the body. Some mental health conditions, however, may develop or stem from a preexisting condition that requires medical intervention. There are also those who have a pre-disposition to addiction to drugs, alcohol, pornography, gambling, and other mind-altering activities. Seeking experts in these fields of psychology and therapy while committing to spiritual practice/discipline can create a path that puts you in the captain's seat.

I pray for people struggling with mental issues every day—that they can be diagnosed effectively and correctly, but also not negate the spiritual practice I believe is essential.

I had a roommate with a car that only made right-hand turns. The defroster also didn't work, so driving in the winter was a nightmare. I had to roll down the windows even in winter because my breath would fog up the inside of the glass. If it got too cold on the outside, I would have to scrape the ice on the windshield while driving. We had blankets in the car, and to make matters worse, the radio didn't work. If there was a moment where you had no choice but to make a left-hand turn, you would have to turn on the radio which would make the car rattle in such a way that the damaged left-side fender would give just enough to jerk the wheel to the left, allowing for a left-hand turn. Wow! Talk about needing a new vehicle. But we drove it, and it was an adventure.

You may be laughing about this story because you might have your own version, or perhaps it conjures up a different memory. Despite a lot going on with the car, it got us from point A to point B.

At times in life our mental health can feel a lot like that car. There is a lot going on personally, professionally, and physically. Through birth, life choices, or other traumas our life vehicle is broken even if we manage to get from point A to point B. Whether psychological well-being is equivalent to a mental health cold, a life-threatening condition, or anything in between, it is important for you to feel empowered and reach out to mental health professionals.

Putting It All into Practice

After nearly two years of being dedicated only to my spiritual practices, the trunk and foundation of my being, my mental fortitude had been rejuvenated. I seemed able to address unexpected events and challenges with a renewed sense of sturdiness and wisdom. In a step of faith, I decided it was time to put all this visualization and meditation to work and face my fear of relationship. For one week I dedicated myself to imagining being married to the woman of my dreams. I felt the feelings of how that would make me feel, and I allowed those feelings to be my prayer. My imagination allowed me to feel the feelings of having a son and the joy that would give me. I imagined the balance of life, the sense of responsibility, and continued to work on myself while learning to love another.

The same week I was also tested on matters of the heart. I was approached by three different women interested in a fling. I politely declined as I was committed to the prayer of my heart. On the third "offer" I remember saying, "I am in a different state of mind. I seek the one whom I can complement and who can complement me."

Her response, "You should meet a consultant for the business I work with. She would be perfect for you."

Not trusting the woman's judgment, I quickly batted the idea away, but my curiosity led me to social media to look up this "perfect for me" person. When I laid eyes on her page and began to read her posts, seeing but a small window into her life, I knew that if I was ever going to get married again, this was the person for me. She matched the image in my mind which I had held in my heart for that week.

The events that transpired over the next few months led me to meet this woman, court her, and marry her. I remember how I felt on my first date with her at a local coffee shop. I was so nervous I was afraid to drink caffeine and become a frantic chatter box. But I thought ahead and brought my own decaf tea just in case. When we went to order, she ordered a mint tea with the tea bag on the side, I ordered a hot water. Puzzled, she looked at me, "Just hot water?" I reached in my pocket, and with a quiver in my voice, I said, "I bring my own tea." She looked at me with a gleam in her eyes and a look of awe. She reached into her pocket and said, "So do I." I guess you could say it was love at first tea bag (big smile on my face as I write this).

Reflecting on the dance of courtship with my wife, I recall one of our deeper conversations regarding her inability to conceive children as she knew how important that was to me. In that moment I completely released the desire, trusting in the power of God, the One beyond all understanding. I looked into her eyes and said, "I want to be with you for who you are, not for your ability or inability to have children."

Imagine our surprise—and the doctor's surprise who told her she would never be able to conceive—when she became pregnant. I still have a sense of victory, knowing the same doctor who told her she would never be able to have children is the same doctor who delivered our son.

When I look at my life and all the disbelief I've lived, it took a miracle to believe that I could love, be married, or even have a child. I don't know when those seeds were planted, but they were planted long before I even tried to desire again. I bring this up to show that the miracle of our child happened long before. Somehow, accepting and recognizing that a miracle may never occur, embracing my spiritual practices, and becoming the captain of my circumstances, regardless of the outcome, probably pushed out the unexplainable.

I believe in the impossible. I believe in those miracles. But readiness to embrace those miracles derives from the transformation of the mind through practices, and this is what I want to emphasize. Whether you are waiting for a miracle or life's waters are still, decide to do things that are good spiritual practices for your soul. When you feel like giving up, arise. When you no longer have a purpose to pursue anymore, arise. When life's comforts or contentment have lulled you into inhibition, arise. When you're afraid and lonely, arise. When you're excited seeing the results of hard work, arise and witness things being even greater than you imagined!

Questions to Ask Yourself:

What spiritual practices mentioned or not mentioned would you like to practice and learn more about?

What helps you turn a practice into a discipline and way of life?

Who do you reach out to for help when you notice your health and inner strength deteriorating?

5

BRANCHES

My father has a disease known as multiple sclerosis (MS). I can remember the last time my father could run. I can remember the last time he could walk. By thirteen I was the strongest person in my household and became essential to helping my dad perform everyday tasks.

At first, I saw my dad like Sisyphus from Greek Mythology. Sisyphus was punished by the Greek god Zeus for cheating death. Every day he would have to roll a giant bolder up a hill, only for it to roll back down every time he neared the top. His task: to do this for eternity. Watching my father struggle with MS felt like he was being punished wrongfully. How much strength of character does it take to fight every day a battle that you are slowly losing? I might never fully understand the emotional toll that journey has taken on my father, but I know how it impacted me. I mourned for him. I cried for the things I felt were robbed from my experience growing up with a father in a wheelchair, unable to participate in play that demanded physical strength.

When I was six years old and my father was more noticeably losing his physical abilities, I would escape reality by climbing the huge oak tree across the street from our townhome. This tree had a circumference of at least six feet and towered above all the houses nearby. On the first level, branches spread out like fingers on a hand. There were five branches. When I sat on this level, I felt safe, secure, and protected. Every time I left the tree, that feeling left.

One day I fell asleep in the tree. My father, despite his challenges, managed to get to the tree to call me home for supper. As I leaped out of the tree, I took my father's hand and realized that while holding his hand I felt the same sense of security. I felt safe and protected. Looking up at my father, I understood the tree lived in him. It was a strong tree with branches that covered all who were willing to be under it. I didn't know what it took to have a tree like that inside of me, but I knew I wanted it. I wanted to be just like my dad, the one who could provide far greater than his physical limitations indicated.

My father dedicated his life to ministry and serving others with his love. He devoted his education to urban ministry, looking at how to bring the love of Christ to the inner city. His branches reached out far beyond himself.

Service

The branches are when the foundation of our being is so strong that we spread our faith in a way that it serves others around us.

The foundation, your spiritual practices, elevates you so you can focus on others and inspire their faith. Why? Because you can now recognize the various points in which different aspects of your life are taking shape. Hopefully, through the wisdom of that knowledge, you can recognize the different places people are in and serve them, appreciating the moment they are experiencing. You can inspire their faith and vision, complementing them based on your own experiences. We could argue that service to people is also a spiritual practice, but its intention is to branch out. The growth you are doing when you branch out is different than the disciplines of spiritual practices.

Service can mean the service to one's emotional and mental safety. Doctors, nurses, teachers, pastors, social workers, parents, caregivers, and so on, all serve. When we stop and take the word "sales" out of some job position titles, often that person is trying to direct us to products that serve our needs. Think of when you go to big box stores, who helps you find what you are looking for? Customer service people. They're indeed serving people.

Understanding that in the moment you ask for a customer service rep's assistance, they are supposed to be putting your needs above their own. All those who consciously serve are the gatekeepers providing others access to resources to build their own ships, grow their visions, and become empowered. That, to me, really should always be the American dream. It should always be, "Hey, how do I empower others, serve them, love them?" The labor of our lives, "the job," is rooted in serving others.

A letter of recommendation is a service because you might be providing someone an opportunity, a chance they otherwise would not have been able to receive. Mentorship is stewardship and service by being the gatekeeper of knowledge and wisdom to provide people access to future visions and opportunities they otherwise would never have explored.

The military was one way I served others. To serve our country is to love our country, and to love our country is to serve it. To be a patriot means to have an allegiance to your country so strong that you're willing to serve it above your own desires in life.

As I served in the military, I was able to love people out of a sense of duty, respect, honor, integrity, and personal courage. It was an environment where I could love people in different stages of their lives. We were trained and fine-tuned to provide different versions of love. We were more than just a sergeant or an officer screaming. We were teachers, mentors, leaders, and friends.

Many of my peers who did basic training with me learned to have an affection for the screams of our instructors. It's true our training induced pain and fear, even stress at the initial stage, but we became immune to its coarseness because we recognized it as love—it was meant to teach, shape, and prepare us for the storms. It was designed to inspire us so we could excel beyond the storms. If not, many would be crushed by the type of storms we were expected to face.

One of my positions in the military was a chaplain assistant. I often worked with those who had been shipwrecked. It was so disheartening looking at people who didn't know who to trust and how to trust and were becoming shipwrecked. The work was endless, but equipped with the desire to serve, I worked tirelessly searching for those asking for help and not getting it. Our mission: find all the shipwrecks, including those who were drowning or even capsizing, and speak life into them.

In order to speak life into people, my tongue, like a sharp knife, imitated the delicate process of a surgeon surgically cutting out the lies that intertwined themselves in people's lives. What is collected in the darkness and the soil stage of our lives will also grow with the seed when the time comes due. It can choke life out of our tree like a vine so embedded that to remove it will leave a divide where it once had so closely attached itself.

The task of unraveling embedded lies involves a patient heart and listening with every fiber of compassion. I see this as the dark side of our souls, the parts we allowed to grow with the seeds of opportunities.

As I reflect on my own journey, as well as those I have crossed paths with, I have seen moments where we spend more time fighting the invisible enemy inside than living a life of freedom. Could you imagine if the energy of fighting internal struggles were directed toward achieving goals instead?

For me, my service was the bond I had for my country as a serviceman. It was the work I did out of the deep love I have for people. My sense of duty and responsibility to love others emerged as I learned to love myself. It was the idea that providing for and serving others is what it means to be American and to truly put the needs of my country above my own, regardless of circumstances at home, relationships, and even my financial situation. It was a devotion to my peers and theirs to me. It was from this dedication to the mission that I was willing to serve even to the detriment of myself. This was a sacrifice I did not fully understand until later in life.

At the end of my service, I was emotionally broke because I had stretched myself so far out, further than my trunk could support, so my tree branches were just falling on the ground. I had to trim myself way back, taking out all the serving of others so the trunk could grow upright again. I felt like there was nothing left of me to give. Upon reflection, I was particularly vulnerable during that first year back from my deployment. I had stretched out a hand when my comrades were hurting, experiencing trauma, having life challenges at the home front, and when they had thoughts of suicide. Now I was home alone. I felt emotionally crippled, lost in my own pains and fears, trying to redefine my purpose. Some call this feeling burnout or compassion fatigue.

This is one of the few moments in my life that I wished I had healthy friends who weren't facing the same "coming back" challenges I was. I may have processed things differently; I may have found a new way to be rejuvenated. I may have made different decisions that aided to growing in healthy ways.

Questions to Ask Yourself:

How do you serve others and branch out?

What ways do you rejuvenate yourself when you feel burned out?

What is the most rewarding aspect to you in the ways you serve or express love?

6
FRUIT

The abundant blessings from all the growth and hard work are ready now! Leaves emerge from the living waters carried up from the roots through the trunk and branches. The sun and God's blessings from above expose vibrant green growth and fruit! It is the expression of our spiritual health and faith development.

Some may recognize this as the law of correspondence from the hermetic principles. The law of correspondence states that as above, so below, and as below, so above. The concept is that the emotional work of building from nothing or bringing into existence and the hard labor of embracing spiritual practices as part of your every day bring you to a place where you can visually see the reciprocal relationship God is having in your physical life.

More than the fruits of labor, God's blessing takes the works we have done and multiplies the impact beyond our anticipation and vision.

I often think of this as one of the most exciting parts of our faith journey. This synergy with God to me feels a lot like when I was a kid, and it was my birthday. It feels like everything is going to go my way or that the universe is collaborating, conspiring for my benefit.

As magnificent as this feeling is, I struggled with allowing God's abundance in my life. I was so dedicated to growing taller and stronger that the idea of bearing fruit and touching lives in such a way was scary. I understood the feeling of surviving, but to thrive felt like a vulnerable place. To reconcile with this fear, I needed to learn more about abundance and how it relates to the fruit we produce in life.

Abundance

Growing up as a pastor's kid, the idea of abundance was a bit of a foreign concept. We had a place to live, we had enough clothes, we had one pair of sneakers, one pair of church shoes, and a pair of slippers. On rare occasions we might have sandals. I didn't notice anything lacking in my life, neither did I notice plenty or excess. As a result, as I got older, the idea of having plenty or excess seemed wasteful. Anything I purchased had to be a legitimized need. I felt guilty for wanting more than enough. Imagine the mental struggle and overthinking every time I purchased something. Did I pay too much? Was this item really necessary?

While I think it is important to keep wants and needs in perspective, I struggled deeply every time I saw a reference to abundance in the Bible, which occurs more than seventy times! How is it that God had called me to live life abundantly, and yet, I didn't feel like I was experiencing it?

I was equally excited about abundance as I was afraid. What if I had more than enough money, clothes, shoes, or gadgets? How would I feel? What would it feel like to have financial security? I decided to meditate on the idea of abundance. I wanted to rid my mind of any sense of scarcity or negative thoughts that hindered my attempt to embrace and receive abundance.

During this stage of learning, doubt continued to rule my thoughts. On one hand I found myself with more opportunities in friendships, experiences, and work that offered many of my heart's desires. Rather than feeling grateful, internally I was seized, uncertain of which direction to pursue. Which way was the right way to go? The "what ifs" kept me up at night. What if I took that new job? What if I moved? What if I signed up for being a member of this board? What if I coached youth sports? What if I didn't have enough time? What if I couldn't keep up with all of my commitments? I spent hours calculating the perceived outcomes and consequences.

And I was miserable.

I was more concerned with making choices than appreciating the opportunities. I was *not* coming from a place of discernment and wisdom but a form of self-sabotage. As new and exciting ventures, ideas, and possibilities would arise, I would invite negative thinking. that snowballed into more negative thought for the rest of the day. I continued to find the negative in everything I did.

Fruit

When I chose to embrace the possibilities, to dream and imagine, I was better able to discern my heart, my joy, and my passions. Pouring out of me was an abundance of joy, gratitude, love, and peace—the fruit of the Spirit referenced in Galatians 5. And pouring into me were God's love and blessings. Everything I did was ten times more successful than what I could even imagine. There was this effortless flow of resources for every project I did.

For example, I had been exploring the possibility of purchasing a home. Three days after I put an offer in, my current home caught fire. The insurance paid to clean all my belongings and even brought them to my new home. During that time our family was blessed with grants and ministries which helped to provide the resources to build a handicap accessible in-law suite to the new home for my parents to be better accommodated. The house was on a once-functional cattle farm, which also had served as a landing site of over fifty years of garbage in the back yard. Teens, neighbors, and volunteer groups came and helped remove four forty-yard dumpsters of trash and over two thousand tires.

Looking back, it seems like magic. What could have been a trying time filled with worry, turned into an abundant time with countless blessings. Every challenge I faced during that six-month transition was met with an overwhelming joyful experience and reminder of God's love.

What is the purpose of fruit? In 1 Corinthians 13, it talks about how we can have all sorts of gifts and talents, but without love, it is nothing, meaningless. Fruit, specifically the fruit of the Spirit, and all the abundant blessings coming from God in conjunction with the hard work we have done in our lives, is meant to continue the work of love.

Fruit has its seasons in our life and is a constant aspect of regrowing and developing our faith. The fullness of the experience cannot take place if we limit God's abundance and love. I believe that the act of dedicating the work we do to God is inviting God to multiply our fruit and the abundant blessings that serve us and others. Receive it, embrace it, and be thankful.

Questions to Ask Yourself:

Where do you see abundance in your life?

What challenges do you see with accepting God's blessings in your life?

What ways have you provided or benefited from others' fruits?

PRUNING

Now that we have taken full ownership of the direction of our life, we still need to maintain our faith, growth, and actions. We still need to have spiritual practices and disciplines; we still need to investigate the difficult-to-understand parts. We may need to off-board habits and ideas we have carried which no longer serve the life we now live with the faith we have developed and abundant fruit we produce.

Pruning is the process of investigating our passions and inspecting what we allow to grow in our heart. Like the analogy of the tree, pruning is where we cut off dead branches or even perhaps live branches and edges to promote a specific type of growth and direction. We might have to cut off and remove the parts of our lives that may hinder growth or cause us to no longer produce fruit. If we decide not to, life's circumstances will do it. Whichever manner, pruning has to happen, and it will take place in an unprejudiced way. It's important not to misinterpret pruning when it occurs.

God uses various methods to help prune us. Sometimes our own choices and decisions shape our future. Other times our mistakes direct where we go. In another light, we cannot go back and revisit the things we didn't quite conquer or did not experience the success we set out for.

One way I was pruned and would like to evaluate is through moments I have shared with some of the managers I have had throughout my life. My interactions with these individuals placed me in very difficult scenarios where I needed to make hard decisions that called for wisdom. All the situations were painful in some way. These moments, however, continue to shape or prune me and affect the decisions I make, and how I choose to be a leader in my life and in the lives of future leaders I impact.

I was tempted to blame other. Instead, however, I challenged myself to take responsibility for what I could and chose to grow rather than becoming entrapped with anger and frustration. As you read these scenarios consider how they make you feel. Observe what questions or details you might want to understand to form a full opinion. Observe how you break down what took place. Was there cultural bias, prejudice, and fear playing a role? Following the scenarios, I will share a short prayer I use in pruning moments.

Scenario 1

I was a young banker sitting in my cubicle with a disgruntled client. Angry at the bank, the client proceeded to spit insults and derogatory statements my way, cursing me out, using racial slurs, and so forth. I could feel the heat escaping my flesh while trying to remain calm. I wanted to draw the line. My manager arrived in a swift and decisive moment. Looking at the person, he handed them a check. I remember his words, "We have the right to refuse business. We have closed your accounts; you are not welcome here. You can leave now, or I can have security escort you." Both shocked and alarmed, the client was caught off guard. In silence he took his check and left.

Scenario 2

I was working in an analyst role at a big corporation, and my boss was on vacation. We were a small team of three employees, and my coworker was out for an appointment. It was lunchtime, and it was usually my custom to go to the break area and have lunch. Instead, I chose to stay at my desk in case during my hour off someone needed me. I sat at my desk eating a banana. My desk was adjustable, and I had my knee pressed against it to lean back in my chair.

Several weeks later I was called to a disciplinary review. Apparently, I had been recorded at my desk. From the angle of the recording, it appeared I had my feet on the desk and didn't take my role seriously. I was in shock. The very action I took to be available was now the action being scrutinized as a reason for disciplinary action.

Scenario 3

I was coming back from a work event one evening and decided to stop at the office to drop off some supplies. As I approached the office, I saw my boss and a woman who was not his wife. The shades were then closed. I decided to go back later, and when I did, the shades were open. My boss was there working on his computer. I thought long and hard. Should I say something? Is it none of my business? My boss mentioned he saw me pull up. There wasn't much else to say. At the time, the only thing I felt confident in saying was, "I won't tell on you, but I can't support your behavior."

Scenario 4

I had just presented a report which provided marketing and product recommendations. My manager, my director, and senior director were all present and seemed very pleased with the effort and thoughtfulness of the recommendations. My senior director patted me on the back and proceeded to say, "Good job, Timmy." I felt belittled. The only person who had ever called me Timmy was my mom. Not wanting to cause a scene, I decided to wait and write an email. When asking my direct manager to review it, he encouraged me not to send it. I still remember him taking a deep pause. He took his glasses off and said, "I want you to consider your career here. It may be much wiser to avoid correcting your senior director and prevent uncertainty in your career. I am speaking from my own experience." Despite holding on to the letter for months, I never sent it.

A Short Prayer

Lord, I am thankful, and I hope that in all my experiences I can recognize you and learn wisdom. I accept being corrected and being challenged. Even in the moments where I feel like I was wronged or incapable of fighting for my own justice, I pray that I focus more on trusting you than sitting in unfruitful emotions. I love you. My heart is yours. My mind is yours. My soul belongs to you. Amen.

Questions to Ask Yourself:

Reflect on your own examples of pruning experiences. Why did it happen?

What was the lesson learned?

In positive ways how did it shape and impact new growth?

FINAL THOUGHTS

While the ideas of producing the tree of your faith are in chronological order, often we have to go back and redevelop parts of our faith journey that did not fully develop. The process tends to be a cycle of different aspects of each growth stage we experience as we tackle new challenges and directions in life.

By recognizing what step you are on, you can refocus your attention and energy toward that in contrast to wondering and unproductive reactions. Setbacks can still happen but that doesn't mean they need to derail us or cause us to desert the growth and faith development we are experiencing.

Grow with God, learn the secrets of your own faith journey, share the stories of triumph, failures, and everything in between. Teach others connected to you and your root system. With abundant faith, growth arises. Drop fruits and blessings of unconditional love all around you.

I urge you to use your faith journey as a call to leadership—not just in your own life but in a way that inspires greatness in others. Imagine how your story can complement the growth of those around you. Maybe you can mentor others, create an accountability group, a spiritual group, or promote a recovery support program. Any of these crowds have persons struggling to create new practices in their lives or who have yet to own their faith, to intentionally grab the reigns of life.

The other benefit to understanding the faith journey and growth stages is that you become more aware of someone's heart when they communicate with you. As you listen, what are they really trying to say? Should you pose a question to recognize the next steps or encourage them to embrace the step they're on?

Complementing through questions proves not only that you heard them, but you become an advocate for their soul. After all, the soul needs to know it is recognized and identified. One African culture greets each other with a phrase that is translated as, "I see you." That's so insightful when we think about how we engage with one another and learn to listen to one another. It is saying, I see you, my brother; I see you, my sister. I see who you are. For someone to recognize who we are validates us, just like we have to almost recognize our sins or failures to move on from them. When people see us, and we allow them to see us for who we are, we can take steps toward what we want to proclaim in our lives.

Being in a faith community helps extend our root system. Just like in life there are many different types of trees—some short or tall, some with long roots and some with shallow roots—an interconnected faith community promotes growth for everyone.

Thank you for listening to some of my story, my thoughts, fears, struggles, and successes. I wanted to write a word of encouragement while being vulnerable and sharing some of myself with you. There are far more struggles I have faced and also far more growth I still need to work on. As I revisit the areas of my life I need to grow in, or I jump into a new challenge, I use these faith development stages: soil, seed, roots, trunk, branches, fruit, and pruning. This focus brings patience, trust, certainty, and an idea of where I should direct my attention as I grow. I have found that emerging into a greater version of myself comes from the faith within me, stretching past where I once was firmly rooted and into the unknown. Tapping into my faith paves the way into a new, uncharted universe where I can explore life with anticipation and a heart of love.

Being an explorer is more than just being inquisitive. It also means that you have the skills and the navigation system to set sail above the clouds. You've come to a certain place of expertise where your confidence says, I've been through this; I've been through swamps. I've experienced being lost in the waters. I've been through the hills and valleys, and I know myself when I face new circumstances. I find my guiding stars, my map, and my direction. I am the captain of my faith. I choose to arise, once more, again and again.

About the Author

After nearly ten years of military service, Timothy Frazier settled in the countryside of Michigan with his wife, son, energetic dog, Rocky, and obsessively hungry cat, Al. He loves that he has been able to create a space for his parents to live with them as one family unit. While Tim continues to work his job in the finance sector, he still finds time to write inspirational books and children's stories. He aspires to teach, motivate, and serve others, empowering them to strive past the unknown and to explore their passions.